Writing Idiomatic Python

Jeff Knupp

2013

Copyright 2013 by Jeff Knupp

All rights reserved.

No part of this book may be reproduced in any form or by any electronic or mechanical means without permission in writing from the author.

Jeff Knupp Visit me at www.jeffknupp.com

Preface

There's a famous old quote about writing maintainable software:

```
Always code as if the guy who ends up maintaining your code will be a violent
psychopath who knows where you live.
--John Woods comp.lang.c++
```

While I'm not usually one for aphorisms, this one strikes a cord with me. Maybe it's because I've spent my professional career writing software at huge companies, but I have yet to inherit code that didn't eventually cause me to curse the original author at some point. Everyone (besides you, of course, dear reader) struggles to write code that's easy to maintain. When Python became popular, many thought that, because of its terseness, it would naturally lead to more maintainable software.

Alas, maintainability is not an emergent property of using an expressive language. Badly written Python code is just as unmaintainable as badly written C++, Perl, Java and all the rest of the languages known for their, *ahem*, readability. Terse code is not a free lunch.

So what do we do? Resign ourselves to maintaining code we can't understand? Rant on Twitter and The Daily WTF about the awful code we have to work on? What must we do to stop the pain?

Write. Idiomatic. Code.

It's that simple. Idioms in a programming language are a sort of lingua franca to let future readers know exactly what we're trying to accomplish. We may document our code extensively, write exhaustive unit tests, and hold code reviews three times a day, but the

PREFACE

fact remains: when someone else needs to make changes, the code is king. If that someone is you, all the documentation in the world won't help you understand unreadable code. After all, how can you even be sure the code is doing what the documentation says?

We're usually reading someone else's code because there's a problem. But idiomatic code helps here, too. Even if it's wrong, when code is written idiomatically, it's far easier spot bugs. Idiomatic code reduces the cognitive load on the reader. After learning a language's idioms, you'll spend less time wondering "Wait, why are they using a named tuple there" and more time understanding what the code actually does.

After you learn and internalize a language's idioms, reading the code of a like-minded developer feels like speed reading. You're no longer stopping at every line, trying to figure out what it does while struggling to keep in mind what came before. Instead, you'll find yourself almost skimming the code, thinking things like 'OK, open a file, transform the contents to a sorted list, generate the giant report in a thread-safe way.' When you have that level of insight into code someone else wrote, there's no bug you can't fix and no enhancement you can't make.

All of this sounds great, right? There's only one catch: you have to know and use a language's idioms to benefit. Enter Writing Idiomatic Python. What started as a hasty blog post of idioms (fueled largely by my frustration while fixing the code of experienced developers new to Python) is now a full-fledged eBook.

I hope you find the book useful. It is meant to be a living document, updated in near-real time with corrections, clarifications, and additions. If you find an error in the text or have difficulty deciphering a passage, please feel free to email me at jeff@jeffknupp.com. With their permission, I'll be adding the names of all who contribute bug fixes and clarifications to the appendix.

Cheers,

Jeff Knupp

January, 2013

Change List

Version 1.1, February 2, 2013

- **New idiom:** "Use `sys.exit` in your script to return proper error codes" idiom
- Greatly expanded discussion in "Avoid comparing directly to True, False, or None" and added mention of comparison to None when checking if optional arguments were set (to match the idiom "Avoid using ", [], and {} as default parameters to functions".
- Expanded "Use the `* operator` to represent the"rest" of a list" idiom expanded with additional cases
- Fixed page numbering issue causing numbers in table of contents and index not to match the text
- Fixed various typos and grammatical changes
- Changed font size and various layout issues (some of which caused text to run off the page
- Changed preface text

Contents

Preface	iii
Change List	v
Version 1.1, February 2, 2013	v
Contents	v
1 Control Structures and Functions	**1**
1.1 For loops	1
1.1.1 Use the `enumerate` function in loops instead of creating an "index" variable	1
1.1.2 Use the `in` keyword to iterate over an `iterable`	3
1.1.3 Use `else` to execute code after a `for` loop concludes	4
1.2 Functions	6
1.2.1 Avoid using `''`, `[]`, and `{}` as `default parameters` to functions	6
1.2.2 Use `*args` and `**kwargs` to accept arbitrary arguments	8
1.3 If Statements	11
1.3.1 Avoid placing conditional branch code on the same line as the colon	11
1.3.2 Avoid repeating variable name in compound `if` statement	12
1.3.3 Avoid comparing directly to `True`, `False`, or `None`	13
2 Working with Data	**16**
2.1 Classes	16
2.1.1 Define `__str__` in a class to show a human-readable representation	16

CONTENTS

	2.1.2	Use underscores in function and variable names to help mark "private" data	18
2.2	Dictionaries		22
	2.2.1	Use the `default` parameter of `dict.get` to provide default values	22
	2.2.2	Use a `dict comprehension` to build a `dict` clearly and efficiently	23
2.3	Lists		24
	2.3.1	Use a `list comprehension` to create a transformed version of an existing list	24
	2.3.2	Use the `*` operator to represent the "rest" of a list	25
2.4	Strings		26
	2.4.1	Chain `string` functions to make a simple series of transformations more clear	26
	2.4.2	Use `''.join` when creating a single `string` for `list` elements	27
	2.4.3	Prefer the `format` function for formatting strings	28
2.5	Tuples		30
	2.5.1	Use `tuples` to unpack data	30
	2.5.2	Use `_` as a placeholder for data in a tuple that should be ignored	31
2.6	Variables		32
	2.6.1	Avoid using a temporary variable when performing a `swap` of two values	32
2.7	Generators		33
	2.7.1	Prefer a `generator expression` to a `list comprehension` for simple iteration	33
	2.7.2	Use a `generator` to lazily load infinite sequences	34
2.8	Context Managers		36
	2.8.1	Use a `context manager` to ensure resources are properly managed	36
2.9	Sets		37
	2.9.1	Understand and use the mathematical `set` operations	37
	2.9.2	Use a `set comprehension` to generate sets concisely	39
	2.9.3	Use sets to eliminate duplicate entries from `Iterable` containers	40

3 Organizing Your Code   42
    3.1 Formatting 42

		3.1.1	Use all capital letters when declaring global constant values	42
		3.1.2	Format your code according to `PEP8`	44
		3.1.3	Avoid placing multiple statements on a single line	45
	3.2	Imports		46
		3.2.1	Prefer `absolute imports` to `relative imports`	46
		3.2.2	Do not use `from foo import *` to import the contents of a module.	48
		3.2.3	Arrange your `import` statements in a standard order	49
	3.3	Modules and Packages		51
		3.3.1	Use `modules` for encapsulation where other languages would use Objects	51
	3.4	Executable Scripts		53
		3.4.1	Use the `if __name__ == '__main__'` pattern to allow a file to be both imported and run directly	53
		3.4.2	Use `sys.exit` in your script to return proper error codes	55

4 General Advice — 57

4.1 Avoid Reinventing the Wheel . . . 57
    4.1.1 Get to know `PyPI` (the Python Package Index) . . . 57
    4.1.2 Learn the Contents of the Python Standard Library . . . 59
4.2 Modules of Note . . . 60
    4.2.1 Use functions in the `os.path` module when working with directory paths . . . 60
    4.2.2 Learn the contents of the itertools module . . . 62

5 Contributors — 63

Chapter 1

Control Structures and Functions

1.1 For loops

1.1.1 Use the `enumerate` function in loops instead of creating an "index" variable

Programmers coming from other languages are used to explicitly declaring a variable to track the index of a container in a loop. For example, in C++:

```cpp
for (int i=0; i < container.size(); ++i)
{
    // Do stuff
}
```

In Python, the `enumerate` built-in function handles this role.

1.1.1.1 Harmful

```python
my_container = ['Larry', 'Moe', 'Curly']
index = 0
for element in my_container:
```

```python
    print ('{} {}'.format(index, element))
    index += 1
```

1.1.1.2 Idiomatic

```python
my_container = ['Larry', 'Moe', 'Curly']
for index, element in enumerate(my_container):
    print ('{} {}'.format(index, element))
```

CHAPTER 1. CONTROL STRUCTURES AND FUNCTIONS

1.1.2 Use the `in` keyword to iterate over an `iterable`

Programmers coming from languages lacking a `for_each` style construct are used to iterating over a container by accessing elements via index. Python's `in` keyword handles this gracefully.

1.1.2.1 Harmful

```python
my_list = ['Larry', 'Moe', 'Curly']
index = 0
while index < len(my_list):
    print (my_list[index])
    index += 1
```

1.1.2.2 Idiomatic

```python
my_list = ['Larry', 'Moe', 'Curly']
for element in my_list:
    print (element)
```

1.1.3 Use `else` to execute code after a `for` loop concludes

One of the lesser known facts about Python's `for` loop is that it can include an `else` clause. The `else` clause is executed after the iterator is exhausted, unless the loop was ended prematurely due to a `break` statement. This allows you to check for a condition in a `for` loop, `break` if the condition holds for an element, `else` take some action if the condition did not hold for any of the elements being looped over. This obviates the need for conditional flags in a loop solely used to determine if some condition held.

In the scenario below, we are running a report to check if any of the email addresses our users registered are malformed (users can register multiple addresses). The idiomatic version is more concise thanks to not having to deal with the `has_malformed_email_address` flag. What's more, *even if another programmer wasn't familiar with the* `for` ... `else` *idiom, our code is clear enough to teach them.*

1.1.3.1 Harmful

```python
for user in get_all_users():
    has_malformed_email_address = False
    print ('Checking {}'.format(user))
    for email_address in user.get_all_email_addresses():
        if email_is_malformed(email_address):
            has_malformed_email_address = True
            print ('Has a malformed email address!')
            break
    if not has_malformed_email_address:
        print ('All email addresses are valid!')
```

1.1.3.2 Idiomatic

```python
for user in get_all_users():
    print ('Checking {}'.format(user))
    for email_address in user.get_all_email_addresses():
```

```python
    if email_is_malformed(email_address):
        print ('Has a malformed email address!')
        break
else:
    print ('All email addresses are valid!')
```

1.2 Functions

1.2.1 Avoid using '', [], and {} as **default parameters** to functions

Though this is explicitly mentioned in the Python tutorial, it nevertheless surprises even experienced developers. In short: prefer `names=None` to `names=[]` for default parameters to functions. Below is the Python Tutorial's treatment of the issue.

1.2.1.1 Harmful

```python
# The default value [of a function] is evaluated only once. This makes
# a difference when the default is a mutable object such as a list,
# dictionary, or instances of most classes. For example, the
# following function accumulates the arguments passed to it on
# subsequent calls.
def f(a, L=[]):
    L.append(a)
    return L
print(f(1))
print(f(2))
print(f(3))
# This will print
#
# [1]
# [1, 2]
# [1, 2, 3]
```

1.2.1.2 Idiomatic

```python
# If you don't want the default to be shared between subsequent calls,
# you can write the function like this instead:
```

```python
def f(a, L=None):
    if L is None:
        L = []
    L.append(a)
    return L
print(f(1))
print(f(2))
print(f(3))
# This will print
# [1]
# [2]
# [3]
```

1.2.2 Use `*args` and `**kwargs` to accept arbitrary arguments

Oftentimes, functions need to accept an arbitrary list of `positional parameters` and/or `keyword parameters`, use a subset of them, and forward the rest to another function. Using `*args` and `**kwargs` as parameters allows a function to accept an arbitrary list of positional and arguments, respectively. The *Django* project make extensive use of this idiom.

The idiom is also useful when maintaining backwards compatibility in an API. If our function accepts arbitrary arguments, we are free to add new arguments in a new version while not breaking existing code using fewer arguments. As long as everything is properly documented, the "actual" parameters of a function are not of much consequence.

1.2.2.1 Harmful

```python
def make_api_call(foo, bar, baz):
    if baz in ('Unicorn', 'Oven', 'New York'):
        return foo(bar)
    else:
        return bar(foo)
# I need to add another parameter to `make_api_call`
# without breaking everyone's existing code.
# I have two options...
def so_many_options():
    # I can tack on new parameters, but only if I make
    # all of them optional...
    def make_api_call(foo, bar, baz, qux=None, foo_polarity=None,
                      baz_coefficient=None, quux_capacitor=None,
                      bar_has_hopped=None, true=None, false=None,
                      file_not_found=None):
        # ... and so on ad infinitum
        return file_not_found
def version_graveyard():
```

```python
# ... or I can create a new function each time the signature
# changes.
def make_api_call_v2(foo, bar, baz, qux):
    return make_api_call(foo, bar, baz) - qux
def make_api_call_v3(foo, bar, baz, qux, foo_polarity):
    if foo_polarity != 'reversed':
        return make_api_call_v2(foo, bar, baz, qux)
    return None
def make_api_call_v4(
        foo, bar, baz, qux, foo_polarity, baz_coefficient):
    return make_api_call_v3(
        foo, bar, baz, qux, foo_polarity) * baz_coefficient
def make_api_call_v5(
        foo, bar, baz, qux, foo_polarity,
        baz_coefficient, quux_capacitor):
    # I don't need 'foo', 'bar', or 'baz' anymore, but I have to
    # keep supporting them...
    return baz_coefficient * quux_capacitor
def make_api_call_v6(
        foo, bar, baz, qux, foo_polarity, baz_coefficient,
        quux_capacitor, bar_has_hopped):
    if bar_has_hopped:
        baz_coefficient *= -1
    return make_api_call_v5(foo, bar, baz, qux,
                            foo_polarity, baz_coefficient,
                            quux_capacitor)
def make_api_call_v7(
        foo, bar, baz, qux, foo_polarity, baz_coefficient,
        quux_capacitor, bar_has_hopped, true):
    return true
def make_api_call_v8(
```

```
        foo, bar, baz, qux, foo_polarity, baz_coefficient,
        quux_capacitor, bar_has_hopped, true, false):
    return false
def make_api_call_v9(
        foo, bar, baz, qux, foo_polarity, baz_coefficient,
        quux_capacitor, bar_has_hopped,
        true, false, file_not_found):
    return file_not_found
```

1.2.2.2 Idiomatic

```
def make_api_call(foo, bar, baz):
    if baz in ('Unicorn', 'Oven', 'New York'):
        return foo(bar)
    else:
        return bar(foo)
# I need to add another parameter to `make_api_call`
# without breaking everyone's existing code.
# Easy...
def new_hotness():
    def make_api_call(foo, bar, baz, *args, **kwargs):
        # Now I can accept any type and number of arguments
        # without worrying about breaking existing code.
        baz_coefficient = kwargs['the_baz']
        # I can even forward my args to a different function without
        # knowing their contents!
        return baz_coefficient in new_function(args)
```

1.3 If Statements

1.3.1 Avoid placing conditional branch code on the same line as the colon

Using indentation to indicate scope (like you already do everywhere else in Python) makes it easy to determine what will be executed as part of a conditional statement. `if`, `elif`, and `else` statements should always be on their own line. No code should follow the `:`.

1.3.1.1 Harmful

```python
name = 'Jeff'
address = 'New York, NY'
if name: print(name)
print(address)
```

1.3.1.2 Idiomatic

```python
name = 'Jeff'
address = 'New York, NY'
if name:
    print(name)
print(address)
```

CHAPTER 1. CONTROL STRUCTURES AND FUNCTIONS

1.3.2 Avoid repeating variable name in compound `if` statement

When one wants to check a variable against a number of values, repeatedly listing the variable being checked is unnecessarily verbose. Using an `iterable` makes the code more clear and improves readability.

1.3.2.1 Harmful

```python
is_generic_name = False
name = 'Tom'
if name == 'Tom' or name == 'Dick' or name == 'Harry':
    is_generic_name = True
```

1.3.2.2 Idiomatic

```python
name = 'Tom'
is_generic_name = name in ('Tom', 'Dick', 'Harry')
```

1.3.3 Avoid comparing directly to `True`, `False`, or `None`

For any object, be it a built-in or user defined, there is a "truthiness" associated with the object. When checking if a condition is true, prefer relying on the implicit "truthiness" of the object in the conditional statement. The rules regarding "truthiness" are reasonably straightforward. All of the following are considered `False`:

- `None`
- `False`
- zero for numeric types
- empty sequences
- empty dictionaries
- a value of 0 or `False` returned when either `__len__` or `__nonzero__` is called

Everything else is considered `True` (and thus most things are implicitly `True`). The last condition for determining `False`, by checking the value returned by `__len__` or `__nonzero__`, allows you to define how "truthiness" should work for any class you create.

`if` statements in Python make use of "truthiness" implicitly, and you should too. Instead of checking if a variable `foo` is `True` like this

```
if foo == True:
```

you should simply check `if foo:`.

There are a number of reasons for this. The most obvious is that if your code changes and `foo` becomes an `int` instead of `True` or `False`, your `if` statement still works. But at a deeper level, the reasoning is based on the difference between **equality** and **identity**. Using == determines if two objects have the same value (as defined by their _eq attribute). Using `is` determines if the two objects are *actually the same object.*

Note that while there are cases where `is` works as if it were comparing for equality, these are special cases and shouldn't be relied upon.

As a consequence, avoid comparing directly to `False` and `None` and empty sequences like `[]`, `{}`, and `()`. If a list named `my_list` is empty, calling `if my_list:` will evaluate to `False`.

There *are* times, however, when comparing directly to `None` is not just recommended, but required. A function checking if an argument whose default value is `None` was actually set must compare directly to `None` like so:

```python
def insert_value(value, position=None):
    """Inserts a value into my container, optionally at the
    specified position"""
    if position is not None:
        ...
```

What's wrong with `if position:`? Well, if someone wanted to insert into position `0`, the function would act as if position hadn't been set, since `0` evaluates to `False`. Note the use of `is not`: comparisons against `None` (a singleton in Python) should always use `is` or `is not`, not `==` (from PEP8).

Just let Python's "truthiness" do the work for you.

1.3.3.1 Harmful

```python
def number_of_evil_robots_attacking():
    return 10
def should_raise_shields():
    # "We only raise Shields when one or more giant robots attack,
    # so I can just return that value..."
    return number_of_evil_robots_attacking()
if should_raise_shields() == True:
    raise_shields()
    print('Shields raised')
else:
    print('Safe! No giant robots attacking')
```

1.3.3.2 Idiomatic

```python
def number_of_evil_robots_attacking():
    return 10
def should_raise_shields():
    # "We only raise Shields when one or more giant robots attack,
    # so I can just return that value..."
    return number_of_evil_robots_attacking()
if should_raise_shields():
    raise_shields()
    print('Shields raised')
else:
    print('Safe! No giant robots attacking')
```

Chapter 2

Working with Data

2.1 Classes

2.1.1 Define `__str__` in a class to show a human-readable representation

When defining a class that is likely to be used with `print()`, the default Python representation isn't too helpful. By defining a `__str__` method, you can control how calling `print` on an instance of your class will look.

2.1.1.1 Harmful

```python
class Point():
    def __init__(self, x, y):
        self.x = x
        self.y = y
p = Point(1, 2)
print (p)
# Prints '<__main__.Point object at 0x91ebd0>'
```

2.1.1.2 Idiomatic

```python
class Point():
    def __init__(self, x, y):
        self.x = x
        self.y = y
    def __str__(self):
        return '{0}, {1}'.format(self.x, self.y)
p = Point(1, 2)
print (p)
# Prints '1, 2'
```

2.1.2 Use underscores in function and variable names to help mark "private" data

All attributes of a class, be they data or functions, are inherently "public" in Python. A client is free to add attributes to a class after it's been defined. In addition, if the class is meant to be inherited from, a subclass may unwittingly change an attribute of the base class. Lastly, it's generally useful to be able to signal to users of your class that certain portions are logically public (and won't be changed in a backwards incompatible way) while other attributes are purely internal implementation artifacts and shouldn't be used directly by client code using the class.

A number of widely followed conventions have arisen to make the author's intention more explicit and help avoid unintentional naming conflicts. While the following two idioms are commonly referred to as 'nothing more than conventions,' both of them, in fact, alter the behavior of the interpreter when used.

First, attributes to be 'protected', which are not meant to be used directly by clients, should be prefixed with a single underscore. Second, 'private' attributes not meant to be accessible by a subclass should be prefixed by *two underscores*. Of course, these are (mostly) merely conventions. Nothing would stop a client from being able to access your 'private' attributes, but the convention is so widely used you likely won't run into developers that purposely choose not to honor it. It's just another example of the Python community settling on a single way of accomplishing something.

Before, I hinted that the single and double underscore prefix were more than mere conventions. Few developers are aware of the fact that prepending attribute names in a class *does actually do something*. Prepending a single underscore means that the symbol won't be imported if the '**all**' idiom is used. Prepending two underscores to an attribute name invokes Python's name mangling. This has the effect of making it far less likely someone who subclasses your class will inadvertently replace your class's attribute with something unintended. If `Foo` is a class, the definition `def __bar()` will be 'mangled' to `_classname__attributename`.

2.1.2.1 Harmful

```python
class Foo():
    def __init__(self):
        self.id = 8
        self.value = self.get_value()
    def get_value(self):
        pass
    def should_destroy_earth(self):
        return self.id == 42
class Baz(Foo):
    def get_value(self, some_new_parameter):
        """Since 'get_value' is called from the base class's
        __init__ method and the base class definition doesn't
        take a parameter, trying to create a Baz instance will fail
        """
        pass
class Qux(Foo):
    """We aren't aware of Foo's internals, and we innocently
    create an instance attribute named 'id' and set it to 42. This
    overwrites Foo's id attribute and we inadvertently blow up the earth.
    """
    def __init__(self):
        super(Qux, self).__init__()
        self.id = 42 # No relation to Foo's id, purely coincidental
q = Qux()
b = Baz()   # Raises 'TypeError'
q.should_destroy_earth()   # returns True
q.id == 42   # returns True
```

2.1.2.2 Idiomatic

```python
class Foo():
    def __init__(self):
        """Since 'id' is of vital importance to us, we don't want a
        derived class accidentally overwriting it. We'll prepend
        with double underscores to introduce name mangling.
        """
        self.__id = 8
        self.value = self.__get_value() # Call our 'private copy'
    def get_value(self):
        pass
    def should_destroy_earth(self):
        return self.__id == 42
    # Here, we're storing an 'private copy' of get_value,
    # and assigning it to '__get_value'. Even if a derived class
    # overrides get_value is a way incompatible with ours, we're fine
    __get_value = get_value
class Baz(Foo):
    def get_value(self, some_new_parameter):
        pass
class Qux(Foo):
    def __init__(self):
        """Now when we set 'id' to 42, it's not the same 'id' that
        'should_destroy_earth' is concerned with. In fact, if you inspect
        a Qux object, you'll find it doesn't have an __id attribute. So we
        can't mistakenly change Foo's __id attribute even
        if we wanted to.
        """
        self.id = 42 # No relation to Foo's id, purely coincidental
        super(Qux, self).__init__()
q = Qux()
```

```
b = Baz()   # Works find now
q.should_destroy_earth()   # returns False
q.id == 42   # returns True
with pytest.raises(AttributeError):
    getattr(q, '__id')
```

2.2 Dictionaries

2.2.1 Use the `default` parameter of `dict.get` to provide default values

Often overlooked in the definition of `dict.get` is the `default` parameter. Without using `default` (or the `collections.defaultdict` class), your code will be littered with confusing `if` statements. Remember, strive for clarity.

2.2.1.1 Harmful

```python
log_severity = None
if 'severity' in configuration:
    log_severity = configuration['severity']
else:
    log_severity = 'Info'
```

2.2.1.2 Idiomatic

```python
log_severity = configuration.get('severity', 'Info')
```

2.2.2 Use a `dict comprehension` to build a `dict` clearly and efficiently

The `list comprehension` is a well-known Python construct. Less well known is the `dict comprehension`. Its purpose is identical: to construct a `dict` in place using the widely understood `comprehension` syntax.

2.2.2.1 Harmful

```python
user_email = {}
for user in users_list:
    if user.email:
        user_email[user.name] = user.email
```

2.2.2.2 Idiomatic

```python
user_email = {user.name: user.email
              for user in users_list if user.email}
```

2.3 Lists

2.3.1 Use a `list comprehension` to create a transformed version of an existing list

`list comprehensions`, when used judiciously, increase clarity in code that builds a list from existing data. This is especially true when elements are both checked for some condition *and* transformed in some way.

There are also (usually) performance benefits to using a `list comprehension` (or alternately, a `generator expression`) due to optimizations in the cPython interpreter.

2.3.1.1 Harmful

```python
some_other_list = range(10)
some_list = list()
for element in some_other_list:
    if is_prime(element):
        some_list.append(element + 5)
```

2.3.1.2 Idiomatic

```python
some_other_list = range(10)
some_list = [element + 5
             for element in some_other_list
             if is_prime(element)]
```

2.3.2 Use the * operator to represent the "rest" of a list

Often times, especially when dealing with the arguments to functions, it's useful to extract a few elements at the beginning (or end) of a list while keeping the "rest" for use later. Python 2 has no easy way to accomplish this aside from using slices as shown below. Python 3 allows you to use the * operator on the left hand side of an assignment to represent the rest of a sequence.

2.3.2.1 Harmful

```python
some_list = ['a', 'b', 'c', 'd', 'e']
(first, second, rest) = some_list[0], some_list[1], some_list[2:]
print(rest)
(first, middle, last) = some_list[0], some_list[1:-1], some_list[-1]
print(middle)
(head, penultimate, last) = some_list[:-2], some_list[-2], some_list[-1]
print(head)
```

2.3.2.2 Idiomatic

```python
some_list = ['a', 'b', 'c', 'd', 'e']
(first, second, *rest) = some_list
print(rest)
(first, *middle, last) = some_list
print(middle)
(*head, penultimate, last) = some_list
print(head)
```

2.4 Strings

2.4.1 Chain `string` functions to make a simple series of transformations more clear

When applying a simple sequence of transformations on some datum, *chaining* the calls in a single expression is often more clear than creating a temporary variable for each step of the transformation. Too much chaining, however, can make your code harder to follow. "No more than three chained functions" is a good rule of thumb.

2.4.1.1 Harmful

```
book_info = ' The Three Musketeers: Alexandre Dumas'
formatted_book_info = book_info.strip()
formatted_book_info = formatted_book_info.upper()
formatted_book_info = formatted_book_info.replace(':', ' by')
```

2.4.1.2 Idiomatic

```
book_info = ' The Three Musketeers: Alexandre Dumas'
formatted_book_info = book_info.strip().upper().replace(':', ' by')
```

2.4.2 Use `''.join` when creating a single `string` for `list` elements

It's faster, uses less memory, and you'll see it everywhere anyway. Note that the two quotes represent the delimiter between `list` elements in the `string` we're creating. `''` just means we wish to concatenate the elements with no characters between them.

2.4.2.1 Harmful

```
result_list = ['True', 'False', 'File not found']
result_string = ''
for result in result_list:
    result_string += result
```

2.4.2.2 Idiomatic

```
result_list = ['True', 'False', 'File not found']
result_string = ''.join(result_list)
```

CHAPTER 2. WORKING WITH DATA

2.4.3 Prefer the `format` function for formatting strings

There are three general ways of formatting strings (that is, creating a `string` that is a mix of hard-coded strings and `string` variables). Easily the worst approach is to use the + operator to concatenate a mix of static strings and variables. Using "old-style" string formatting is slightly better. It makes use of a format string and the % operator to fill in values, much like `printf` does in other languages.

The clearest and most idiomatic way to format strings is to use the `format` function. Like old-style formatting, it takes a format string and replaces placeholders with values. The similarities end there, though. With the `format` function, we can use named placeholders, access their attributes, and control padding and string width, among a number of other things. The `format` function makes string formatting clean and concise.

2.4.3.1 Harmful

```python
def get_formatted_user_info_worst(user):
    # Tedious to type and prone to conversion errors
    return 'Name: ' + user.name + ', Age: ' + \
        str(user.age) + ', Sex: ' + user.sex
def get_formatted_user_info_slightly_better(user):
    # No visible connection between the format string placeholders
    # and values to use. Also, why do I have to know the type?
    # Don't these types all have __str__ functions?
    return 'Name: %s, Age: %i, Sex: %c' % (
        user.name, user.age, user.sex)
```

2.4.3.2 Idiomatic

```python
def get_formatted_user_info(user):
    # Clear and concise. At a glance I can tell exactly what the output
    # should be.
```

```python
    return 'Name: {user.name}, Age: {user.age}, Sex: {user.sex}'.format(
        user=user)
```

CHAPTER 2. WORKING WITH DATA

2.5 Tuples

2.5.1 Use **tuples** to unpack data

In Python, it is possible to "unpack" data for multiple assignment. Those familiar with LISP may know this as `desctructuring bind`.

2.5.1.1 Harmful

```
list_from_comma_separated_value_file = ['dog', 'Fido', 10]
animal = list_from_comma_separated_value_file[0]
name = list_from_comma_separated_value_file[1]
age = list_from_comma_separated_value_file[2]
output = ('{name} the {animal} is {age} years old'.format(
    animal=animal, name=name, age=age))
```

2.5.1.2 Idiomatic

```
list_from_comma_separated_value_file = ['dog', 'Fido', 10]
(animal, name, age) = list_from_comma_separated_value_file
output = ('{name} the {animal} is {age} years old'.format(
    animal=animal, name=name, age=age))
```

2.5.2 Use _ as a placeholder for data in a tuple that should be ignored

When setting a `tuple` equal to some ordered data, oftentimes not all of the data is actually needed. Instead of creating throwaway variables with confusing names, use the _ as a placeholder to tell the reader, "This data will be discarded."

2.5.2.1 Harmful

```python
(name, age, temp, temp2) = get_user_info(user)
if age > 21:
    output = '{name} can drink!'.format(name=name)
# "Wait, where are temp and temp2 being used?"
```

2.5.2.2 Idiomatic

```python
(name, age, _, _) = get_user_info(user)
if age > 21:
    output = '{name} can drink!'.format(name=name)
# "Clearly, only name and age are interesting"
```

2.6 Variables

2.6.1 Avoid using a temporary variable when performing a swap of two values

There is no reason to swap using a temporary variable in Python. We can use tuples to make our intention more clear.

2.6.1.1 Harmful

```
foo = 'Foo'
bar = 'Bar'
temp = foo
foo = bar
bar = temp
```

2.6.1.2 Idiomatic

```
foo = 'Foo'
bar = 'Bar'
(foo, bar) = (bar, foo)
```

2.7 Generators

2.7.1 Prefer a `generator expression` to a `list comprehension` for simple iteration

When dealing with a `sequence`, it is common to need to iterate over a slightly modified version of the `sequence` a single time. For example, you may want to print out the first names of all of your users in all capital letters.

Your first instinct should be to build and iterate over the sequence in place. A `list comprehension` seems ideal, but there's an even better Python built-in: a `generator expression`.

The main difference? A `list comprehension` generates a `list` object and fills in all of the elements immediately. For large lists, this can be prohibitively expensive. The `generator` returned by a `generator expression`, on the other hand, generates each element "on-demand". That list of uppercase user names you want to print out? Probably not a problem. But what if you wanted to write out the title of every book known to the Library of Congress? You'd likely run out of memory in generating your `list comprehension`, while a `generator expression` won't bat an eyelash. A logical extension of the way `generator expressions` work is that you can use a them on infinite sequences.

2.7.1.1 Harmful

```python
for uppercase_name in [name.upper() for name in get_all_usernames()]:
    process_normalized_username(uppercase_name)
```

2.7.1.2 Idiomatic

```python
for uppercase_name in (name.upper() for name in get_all_usernames()):
    process_normalized_username(uppercase_name)
```

2.7.2 Use a `generator` to lazily load infinite sequences

Often, it's useful to provide a way to iterate over a `sequence` that's essentially infinite. Other times, you need to provide an interface to a `sequence` that's incredibly expensive to calculate, and you don't want your user sitting on their hands waiting for you to finish building a list.

In both cases, `generators` are your friend. A `generator` is a special type of coroutine which returns an `iterable`. The state of the `generator` is saved, so that the next call into the `generator` continues where it left off. In the examples below, we'll see how to use a `generator` to help in each of the cases mentioned above.

2.7.2.1 Harmful

```python
def get_twitter_stream_for_keyword(keyword):
    """Get's the 'live stream', but only at the moment
    the function is initially called. To get more entries,
    the client code needs to keep calling
    'get_twitter_livestream_for_user'. Not ideal.
    """
    imaginary_twitter_api = ImaginaryTwitterAPI()
    if imaginary_twitter_api.can_get_stream_data(keyword):
        return imaginary_twitter_api.get_stream(keyword)
current_stream = get_twitter_stream_for_keyword('#jeffknupp')
for tweet in current_stream:
    process_tweet(tweet)
# Uh, I want to keep showing tweets until the program is quit.
# What do I do now? Just keep calling get_twitter_stream_for_keyword?
# That seems stupid.
def get_list_of_incredibly_complex_calculation_results(data):
    return [first_incredibly_long_calculation(data),
            second_incredibly_long_calculation(data),
            third_incredibly_long_calculation(data),
```

CHAPTER 2. WORKING WITH DATA

```
        ]
```

2.7.2.2 Idiomatic

```python
def get_twitter_stream_for_keyword(keyword):
    """Now, 'get_twitter_stream_for_keyword' is a generator
    and will continue to generate Iterable pieces of data
    one at a time until 'can_get_stream_data(user)' is
    False (which may be never).
    """
    imaginary_twitter_api = ImaginaryTwitterAPI()
    while imaginary_twitter_api.can_get_stream_data(keyword):
        yield imaginary_twitter_api.get_stream(keyword)
# Because it's a generator, I can sit in this loop until
# the client wants to break out
for tweet in get_twitter_stream_for_keyword('#jeffknupp'):
    if got_stop_signal:
        break
    process_tweet(tweet)
def get_list_of_incredibly_complex_calculation_results(data):
    """A simple example to be sure, but now when the client code
    iterates over the call to
    'get_list_of_incredibly_complex_calculation_results', we only do as
    much work as necessary to generate the current item.
    """

    yield first_incredibly_long_calculation(data)
    yield second_incredibly_long_calculation(data)
    yield third_incredibly_long_calculation(data)
```

2.8 Context Managers

2.8.1 Use a `context manager` to ensure resources are properly managed

Similar to the *RAII* principle in languages like C++ and D, `context managers` (objects meant to be used with the `with` statement) can make resource management both safer and more explicit. The canonical example is file IO.

Take a look at the "Harmful" code below. What happens if `will_always_raise_exception` does, in fact, raise an exception? Since we haven't caught it in the code below, it will propagate up the stack. We've hit an exit point in our code that might have been overlooked, and we now have no way to close the opened file.

There are a number of classes in the standard library that support or use a `context manager`. In addition, user defined classes can be easily made to work with a `context manager` by defining `__enter__` and `__exit__` methods. Functions may be wrapped with `context managers` through the `contextlib` module.

2.8.1.1 Harmful

```python
file_handle = open(path_to_file, 'r')
for line in file_handle.readlines():
    if will_always_raise_exception(line):
        print('No! An Exception!')
```

2.8.1.2 Idiomatic

```python
with open(path_to_file, 'r') as file_handle:
    for line in file_handle:
        if will_always_raise_exception(line):
            print('No! An Exception!')
```

2.9 Sets

2.9.1 Understand and use the mathematical `set` operations

`sets` are an easy to understand data structure. Like a `dict` with keys but no values, the `set` class implements the `Iterable` and `Container` interfaces. Thus, a `set` can be used in a `for` loop or as the subject of an `in` statement.

For programmers who haven't seen a Set data type before, it may appear to be of limited use. Key to understanding their usefulness is understanding their origin in mathematics. Set Theory is the branch of mathematics devoted to the study of sets. Understanding the basic mathematical set operations is the key to harnessing their power.

Don't worry; you don't need a degree in math to understand or use sets. You just need to remember a few simple operations:

Union The set of elements in A, B, or both A and B (written `A | B` in Python).

Intersection The set of elements in both A and B (written `A & B` in Python).

Difference The set of elements in A but not B (written `A - B` in Python).
  *Note: order matters here. `A - B` is not necessarily the same as `B - A`.

Symmetric Difference The set of elements in either A or B, but not both A *and* B (written `A ^ B` in Python).

When working with lists of data, a common task is finding the elements that appear in all of the lists. Any time you need to choose elements from two or more sequences based on properties of sequence membership, **look to use a `set`**.

Below, we'll explore some typical examples.

2.9.1.1 Harmful

```python
def get_both_popular_and_active_users():
    # Assume the following two functions each return a
    # list of user names
    most_popular_users = get_list_of_most_popular_users()
    most_active_users = get_list_of_most_active_users()
    popular_and_active_users = []
    for user in most_active_users:
        if user in most_popular_users:
            popular_and_active_users.append(user)
    return popular_and_active_users
```

2.9.1.2 Idiomatic

```python
def get_both_popular_and_active_users():
    # Assume the following two functions each return a
    # list of user names
    return(set(
        get_list_of_most_active_users()) & set(
            get_list_of_most_popular_users()))
```

CHAPTER 2. WORKING WITH DATA

2.9.2 Use a `set comprehension` to generate sets concisely

The `set comprehension` syntax is relatively new in Python and, therefore, often overlooked. Just as a `list` can be generated using a `list comprehension`, a `set` can be generated using a `set comprehension`. In fact, the syntax is nearly identical (modulo the enclosing characters).

2.9.2.1 Harmful

```python
users_first_names = set()
for user in users:
    users_first_names.add(user.first_name)
```

2.9.2.2 Idiomatic

```python
users_first_names = {user.first_name for user in users}
```

2.9.3 Use sets to eliminate duplicate entries from `Iterable` containers

It's quite common to have a `list` or `dict` with duplicate values. In a `list` of all surnames of employees at a large company, we're bound to encounter common surnames more than once in the list. If we need a list of all the *unique* surnames, we can use a `set` to do the work for us. Three aspects of `sets` make them the perfect answer to our problem:

1. A `set` contains only unique elements
2. Adding an already existing element to a `set` is essentially "ignored"
3. A `set` can be built from any `Iterable` whose elements are hashable

Continuing the example, we may have an existing `display` function that accepts a `sequence` and displays its elements in one of many formats. After creating a `set` from our original `list`, will we need to change our `display` function?

Nope. Assuming our `display` function is implemented reasonably, our `set` can be used as a drop-in replacement for a `list`. This works thanks to the fact that a `set`, like a `list`, is an `Iterable` and can thus be used in a `for` loop, `list comprehension`, etc.

2.9.3.1 Harmful

```python
unique_surnames = []
for surname in employee_surnames:
    if surname not in unique_surnames:
        unique_surnames.append(surname)
def display(elements, output_format='html'):
    if output_format == 'std_out':
        for element in elements:
            print(element)
    elif output_format == 'html':
        as_html = '<ul>'
```

```python
        for element in elements:
            as_html += '<li>{}</li>'.format(element)
        return as_html + '</ul>'
    else:
        raise RuntimeError('Unknown format {}'.format(output_format))
```

2.9.3.2 Idiomatic

```python
unique_surnames = set(employee_surnames)
def display(elements, output_format='html'):
    if output_format == 'std_out':
        for element in elements:
            print(element)
    elif output_format == 'html':
        as_html = '<ul>'
        for element in elements:
            as_html += '<li>{}</li>'.format(element)
        return as_html + '</ul>'
    else:
        raise RuntimeError('Unknown format {}'.format(output_format))
```

Chapter 3

Organizing Your Code

3.1 Formatting

3.1.1 Use all capital letters when declaring global constant values

To distinguish `constants` defined at the module level (or global in a single script) from imported names, use all uppercase letters.

3.1.1.1 Harmful

```python
seconds_in_a_day = 60 * 60 * 24
# ...
def display_uptime(uptime_in_seconds):
    percentage_run_time = (
        uptime_in_seconds/seconds_in_a_day) * 100
    # "Huh!? Where did seconds_in_a_day come from?"
    return 'The process was up {percent} percent of the day'.format(
        percent=int(percentage_run_time))
# ...
uptime_in_seconds = 60 * 60 * 24
display_uptime(uptime_in_seconds)
```

CHAPTER 3. ORGANIZING YOUR CODE

3.1.1.2 Idiomatic

```python
SECONDS_IN_A_DAY = 60 * 60 * 24
# ...
def display_uptime(uptime_in_seconds):
    percentage_run_time = (
        uptime_in_seconds/SECONDS_IN_A_DAY) * 100
    # "Clearly SECONDS_IN_A_DAY is a constant defined
    # elsewhere in this module."
    return 'The process was up {percent} percent of the day'.format(
        percent=int(percentage_run_time))
# ...
uptime_in_seconds = 60 * 60 * 24
display_uptime(uptime_in_seconds)
```

3.1.2 Format your code according to **PEP8**

Python has a language-defined standard set of formatting rules known as PEP8. If you're browsing commit messages on Python projects, you'll likely find them littered with references to PEP8 cleanup. The reason is simple: if we all agree on a common set of naming and formatting conventions, Python code as a whole becomes instantly more accessible to both novice and experienced developers. PEP8 is perhaps the most explicit example of idioms within the Python community. Read the PEP, install a PEP8 style-checking plugin for your editor (they all have one), and start writing your code in a way that other Python developers will appreciate. Listed below are a few examples.

Identifier Type	Format	Example
Class	Camel case	class StringManipulator():
Variable	Words joined by underscore	words_joined_by_underscore = True
Function	Words joined by underscore	def joined_by_underscore(words):
Constant	All uppercase	SECRET_KEY = 42

Table 3.1: *Unless wildly unreasonable, abbreviations should not be used (acronyms are fine if in common use, like 'HTTP')*

Basically everything not listed should follow the variable/function naming conventions of 'Words joined by an underscore'.

3.1.3 Avoid placing multiple statements on a single line

Though the language definition allows one to use ; to delineate statements, doing so without reason makes one's code harder to read. When multiple statements occur on the same line as an `if`, `else`, or `elif`, the situation is even further confused.

3.1.3.1 Harmful

```
if this_is_bad_code: rewrite_code(); make_it_more_readable();
```

3.1.3.2 Idiomatic

```
if this_is_bad_code:
    rewrite_code()
    make_it_more_readable()
```

3.2 Imports

3.2.1 Prefer `absolute imports` to `relative imports`

When importing a module, you have two choices of the import "style" to use: `absolute imports` or `relative imports`. `absolute imports` specify a module's location (like `<package>.<module>.<submodule>`) from a location which is reachable from `sys.path`.

Relative imports specify a module relative to the current module's location on the file system. If you are the module `package.sub_package.module` and need to `import package.other_module`, you can do so using the dotted `relative import` syntax: `from ..other_module import foo`. A single `.` represents the current package a module is contained in (like in a file system). Each additional `.` is taken to mean "the parent package of", one level per dot. Note that `relative imports` must use the `from ... import ...` style. `import foo` is always treated as an absolute import.

Alternatively, using an `absolute import` you would write `import package.other_module` (possibly with an `as` clause to alias the module to a shorter name.

Why, then, should you prefer absolute imports to relative? Relative imports clutter a module's namespace. By writing `from foo import bar`, you've bound the name `bar` in your module's namespace. To those reading your code, it will not be clear where `bar` came from, especially if used in a complicated function or large module. `foo.bar`, however, makes it perfectly clear where `bar` is defined. The Python programming FAQ goes so far as to say, "Never use relative package imports."

3.2.1.1 Harmful

```
# My location is package.sub_package.module
# and I want to import package.other_module.
# The following should be avoided:
from ...package import other_module
```

3.2.1.2 Idiomatic

```python
# My location is package.sub_package.another_sub_package.module
# and I want to import package.other_module.
# Either of the following are acceptable:
import package.other_module
import package.other_module as other
```

3.2.2 Do not use `from foo import *` to import the contents of a module.

Considering the previous idiom, this one should be obvious. Using an asterisk in an import (as in `from foo import *`) is an easy way to clutter your namespace. This may even cause issues if there are clashes between names you define and those defined in the package.

But what if you have to import a number of names from the `foo` package? Simple. Make use of the fact that parenthesis can be used to group import statements. You won't have to write 10 lines of import statements from the same module, and your namespace remains (relatively) clean.

Better yet, simply use `absolute imports`. If the package/module name is too long, use an `as` clause to shorten it.

3.2.2.1 Harmful

```
from foo import *
```

3.2.2.2 Idiomatic

```
from foo import (bar, baz, qux,
    quux, quuux)
# or even better...
import foo
```

3.2.3 Arrange your `import` statements in a standard order

As projects grow (especially those using web frameworks), so do the number of import statements. Stick *all* of your `import` statements at the top of each file, choose a standard order for your import statements, and stick with it. While the actual ordering is not as important, the following is the order recommended by Python's Programming FAQ:

1. standard library modules
2. third-party library modules installed in site-packages
3. modules local to the current project

Many choose to arrange the imports in (roughly) alphabetical order. Others think that's ridiculous. In reality, it doesn't matter. What matters it that you *do* choose a standard order (and follow it of course).

3.2.3.1 Harmful

```python
import os.path
# Some function and class definitions, one of which uses os.path
# ....
import concurrent.futures
from flask import render_template
# Stuff using futures and Flask's render_template
# ....
from flask import (Flask, request, session, g, redirect, url_for, abort,
    render_template, flash, _app_ctx_stack)
import requests
# Code using flask and requests
# ....
if __name__ == '__main__':
    # Imports when imported as a module are not so
    # costly that they need to be relegated to inside
```

```
    # an 'if __name__ == '__main__'' block...
    import this_project.utilities.sentient_network as skynet
    import this_project.widgets
    import sys
```

3.2.3.2 Idiomatic

```
# Easy to see exactly what my dependencies are and where to make changes
# if a module or package name changes
import concurrent.futures
import os.path
import sys
from flask import (Flask, request, session, g, redirect, url_for, abort,
    render_template, flash, _app_ctx_stack)
import requests
import this_project.utilities.sentient_network as skynet
import this_project.widgets
```

3.3 Modules and Packages

3.3.1 Use `modules` for encapsulation where other languages would use Objects

While Python certainly supports Object Oriented programming, it does not *require* it. Most experienced Python programmers (and programmers in general using a language that facilitates it) use `classes` and `polymorphism` relatively sparingly. There are a number of reasons why.

Most data that would otherwise stored in a `class` can be represented using the simple `list`, `dict`, and `set` types. Python has a wide variety of built-in functions and standard library modules optimized (both in design and implementation) to interact with them. One can make a compelling case that classes should be used only when necessary and almost never at API boundaries.

In Java, classes are the basic unit of encapsulation. Each file represents a Java class, regardless of whether that makes sense for the problem at hand. If I have a handful of utility functions, into a "Utility" class they go! If we don't intuitively understand what it means to be a "Utility" object, no matter. Of course, I exaggerate, but the point is clear. Once one is forced to make everything a class, it is easy to carry that notion over to other programming languages.

In Python, groups of related functions and data are naturally encapsulated in `modules`. If I'm using an MVC web framework to build "Chirp", I may have a package named `chirp` with `model`, `view`, and `controller` modules. If "Chirp" is an especially ambitious project and the code base is large, those modules could easily be `packages` themselves. The `controller` package may have a `persistence` module and a `processing` module. Neither of those need be related in any way other than the sense that they intuitively belong under `controller`.

If all of those modules became classes, interoperability immediately becomes an issue. We must carefully and precisely determine the methods we will expose publicly, how state will be updated, and the way in which our class supports testing. And instead of a `dict` or `list`, we have `Processing` and `Persistence` objects we must write code to support.

Note that nothing in the description of "Chirp" necessitates the use of any classes. Simple `import` statements make code sharing and encapsulation easy. Passing state explicitly as arguments to functions keeps everything loosely coupled. And it becomes far easier to receive, process, and transform data flowing through our system.

To be sure, classes may be a cleaner or more natural way to represent some "things". In many instances, `Object Oriented Programming` is a handy paradigm. Just don't make it the *only* paradigm you use.

3.4 Executable Scripts

3.4.1 Use the `if __name__ == '__main__'` pattern to allow a file to be both imported and run directly

Unlike the `main()` function available in some languages, Python has no built-in notion of a main entry point. Rather, the interpreter immediately begins executing statements upon loading a Python source file. If you want a file to function both as an importable Python module and a stand-alone script, use the `if __name__ == '__main__'` idiom.

3.4.1.1 Harmful

```python
import sys
import os
FIRST_NUMBER = float(sys.argv[1])
SECOND_NUMBER = float(sys.argv[2])
def divide(a, b):
    return a/b
# I can't import this file (for the super
# useful 'divide' function) without the following
# code being executed.
if SECOND_NUMBER != 0:
    print(divide(FIRST_NUMBER, SECOND_NUMBER))
```

3.4.1.2 Idiomatic

```python
import sys
import os
def divide(a, b):
    return a/b
# Will only run if script is executed directly,
# not when the file is imported as a module
```

```python
if __name__ == '__main__':
    first_number = float(sys.argv[1])
    second_number = float(sys.argv[2])
    if second_number != 0:
        print(divide(first_number, second_number))
```

3.4.2 Use `sys.exit` in your script to return proper error codes

Python scripts should be good shell citizens. It's tempting to jam a bunch of code after the `if __name__ == '__main__'` statement and not return anything. Avoid this temptation.

Create a `main` function that contains the code to be run as a script. Use `sys.exit` in `main` to return error codes if something goes wrong or zero if everything runs to completion. The only code under the `if __name__ == '__main__'` statement should call `sys.exit` with the return value of your `main` function as the parameter.

By doing this, we allow the script to be used in Unix pipelines, to be monitored for failure without needing custom rules, and to be called by other programs safely.

3.4.2.1 Harmful

```python
if __name__ == '__main__':
    import sys
    # What happens if no argument is passed on the command line?
    if len(sys.argv) > 1:
        argument = sys.argv[1]
        result = do_stuff(argument)
        # Again, what if this is False? How would other programs know?
        if result:
            do_stuff_with_result(result)
```

3.4.2.2 Idiomatic

```python
def main():
    import sys
    if len(sys.argv) < 2:
        # Calling sys.exit with a string automatically prints the
        # string to stderr and exits with a value of '1' (error)
        sys.exit('You forgot to pass an argument')
    argument = sys.argv[1]
```

```python
    result = do_stuff(argument)
    if not result:
        sys.exit(1)  # We can also exit with just the return code
    do_stuff_with_result(result)
    # Optional, since the return value without this return statment would
    # default to None, which sys.exit treats as 'exit with 0'
    return 0
# The three lines below are the canonical script entry point lines. You'l
# see them often in other Python scripts
if __name__ == '__main__':
    sys.exit(main())
```

Chapter 4

General Advice

4.1 Avoid Reinventing the Wheel

4.1.1 Get to know `PyPI` (the Python Package Index)

If Python's standard library doesn't have a package relevant to your particular problem, the chances are good that PyPI does. As of this writing, there are over **27,000** packages maintained in the index. If your looking to accomplish a particular task and can't find a relevant package in PyPI, chances are it doesn't exist.

The index is fully searchable and contains both Python 2 and Python 3 based packages. Of course, not all packages are created equal (or equally maintained), so be sure to check when the package was last updated. A package with documentation hosted externally on a site like ReadTheDocs is a good sign, as is one for which the source is available on a site like GitHub or Bitbucket.

Now that you found a promising looking package, how do you install it? By far the most popular tool to manage third party packages is pip. A simple `pip install <package name>` will download the latest version of the package and install it in your `site-packages` directory. If you need the bleeding edge version of a package, `pip` is also capable of installing directly from a DVCS like `git` or `mercurial`.

If you create a package that seems generally useful, strongly consider giving back to the Python community by publishing it to PyPI. Doing so is a straightforward process, and future developers will (hopefully) thank you.

4.1.2 Learn the Contents of the Python Standard Library

Part of writing idiomatic code is making liberal use of the standard library. Code that unknowingly reimplements functionality in the standard library is perhaps the clearest signal of a novice Python programmer. Python is commonly said to come with "batteries included" for a good reason. The standard library contains packages covering a wide range of domains.

Making use of the standard library has two primary benefits. Most obviously, you save yourself a good deal of time when you don't have to implement a piece of functionality from scratch. Just as important is the fact that those who read or maintain your code will have a much easier time doing so if you use packages familiar to them.

Remember, the purpose of learning and writing idiomatic Python is to write clear, maintainable, and bug-free code. Nothing ensures those qualities in your code more easily than reusing code written and maintained by core Python developers. As bugs are found and fixed in the standard library, your code improves with each Python release without you lifting a finger.

4.2 Modules of Note

4.2.1 Use functions in the `os.path` module when working with directory paths

When writing simple command-line scripts, new Python programmers often perform herculean feats of string manipulation to deal with file paths. Python has an entire module dedicated to functions on path names: `os.path`. Using `os.path` reduces the risk of common errors, makes your code portable, and makes your code much easier to understand.

4.2.1.1 Harmful

```python
from datetime import date
import os
filename_to_archive = 'test.txt'
new_filename = 'test.bak'
target_directory = './archives'
today = date.today()
os.mkdir('./archives/' + str(today))
os.rename(
    filename_to_archive,
    target_directory + '/' + str(today) + '/' + new_filename)
    today) + '/' + new_filename)
```

4.2.1.2 Idiomatic

```python
from datetime import date
import os
current_directory = os.getcwd()
filename_to_archive = 'test.txt'
new_filename = os.path.splitext(filename_to_archive)[0] + '.bak'
target_directory = os.path.join(current_directory, 'archives')
```

```python
today = date.today()
new_path = os.path.join(target_directory, str(today))
if (os.path.isdir(target_directory)):
    if not os.path.exists(new_path):
        os.mkdir(new_path)
    os.rename(
        os.path.join(current_directory, filename_to_archive),
        os.path.join(new_path, new_filename))
```

4.2.2 Learn the contents of the itertools module

If you frequent sites like StackOverflow, you may notice that the answer to questions of the form "Why doesn't Python have the following obviously useful library function?" almost always references the `itertools` module. The functional programming stalwarts that `itertools` provides should be seen as fundamental building blocks. What's more, the documentation for `itertools` has a 'Recipes' section that provides idiomatic implementations of common functional programming constructs, all created using the itertools module. For some reason, a vanishingly small number of Python developers seem to be aware of the 'Recipes' section and, indeed, the `itertools` module in general (hidden gems in the Python documentation is actually a recurring theme). Part of writing idiomatic code is knowing when you're reinventing the wheel.

Chapter 5

Contributors

I actively solicit feedback on bugs, typos, grammatical and spelling errors, and unclear portions of the text. The following **awesome** individuals have greatly helped improve the quality of this text.

- R. Daneel Olivaw
- Jonathon Capps
- Michael G. Lerner
- Daniel Smith
- Arne Sellmann

Index

''.join, 27
* operator, 25
**kwargs, 8
*args, 8
+, 28
==, 13
_, 31
__enter__, 36
__exit__, 36
__len__, 13
__nonzero__, 13
__str__, 16
_eq, 13

absolute imports, 46, 48
as, 46, 48

bar, 46
break, 4

class, 51
classes, 51
collections.defaultdict, 22
comprehension, 23
constants, 42

Container, 37
context manager, 36
context managers, 36
contextlib, 36

default, 22
default parameters, 6
desctructuring bind, 30
dict, 23, 37, 40, 51
dict comprehension, 23
dict.get, 22

elif, 11, 45
else, 4, 11, 45
enumerate, 1
equality, 13

False, 13, 14
for, 4, 37, 40
format, 28

generator, 33, 34
generator expression, 24, 33

identity, 13
if, 11–13, 45

INDEX

if __name__ == '__main__', 53, 55
import, 46, 49, 52
import *, 48
in, 3, 37
is, 13
Iterable, 37, 40
iterable, 3, 12, 34
itertools, 62

keyword parameters, 8

list, 27, 33, 39, 40, 51, 52
list comprehension, 23, 24, 33, 39, 40

main, 55
modules, 51

None, 13, 14

Object Oriented Programming, 52
os.path, 60

packages, 51
PEP8, 44
polymorphism, 51
positional parameters, 8
print, 16
PyPI, 57

relative imports, 46

sequence, 25, 33, 34, 40
set, 37, 39, 40, 51
set comprehension, 39
string, 26–28

swap, 32
sys.exit, 55

True, 13
tuple, 31
tuples, 30

with, 36

Made in the USA
Lexington, KY
16 February 2013